FOCUS ON FISH

Stephen Savage

Gareth Stevens
Publishing

Please visit our website, www.garethstevens.com.
For a free color catalogue of all our high-quality books,
call toll free 1-800-542-2595 or fax 1-877-542-2596.

Library in Congress Cataloging-in-Publication Data

Savage, Stephen, 1965-
Focus on fish / Stephen Savage.
    p. cm. — (Animal watch)
Includes index.
ISBN 978-1-4339-5984-4 (library binding)
1. Fishes—Juvenile literature. I. Title.
QL617.2.S294 2011
597—dc22

                                2010049249

This edition first published in 2012 by
Gareth Stevens Publishing
111 East 14th Street, Suite 349
New York, NY 10003

Copyright © 2012 Wayland/Gareth Stevens Publishing

Editorial Director: Kerri O'Donnell
Design Director: Haley Harasymiw

Printed in China
CPSIA compliance information: Batch #WAS11GS: For further information contact Gareth Stevens, New York, New York at 1-800-542-2595.

Contents

What a Difference!

There are about 22,000 different types of fish in the world. They come in all sizes, shapes, and colors.

Although a goldfish looks very different from a shark, they are both types of fish. They have some of the same basic features.

↓ The whale shark is 60 feet (18 m) long—the largest fish in the world. It eats small fish and plankton, sucking them into its enormous mouth.

↑ The leafy sea dragon looks like a piece of seaweed. This camouflage helps to protect it from attack.

FISH CHARACTERISTICS

- All fish live in water.
- Fish have scaly skin.
- Fish breathe with gills.
- Fish have fins and a tail.
- Most fish have a swim bladder to help them float.

Simple key to the Animal Kingdom

Invertebrates

Vertebrates

Worms

Snails

Spiders

Insects

Fish

Amphibians

Reptiles

Birds

Mammals

Invertebrates are animals that do not have a backbone.
Vertebrates are animals that have a backbone.

Where do mammals live?

Two-thirds of the earth's surface is covered in water. Fish live in all the world's seas and oceans. Their habitats include the sandy seabed, coral reefs, and underwater forests.

FISH AND DIFFERENT HABITATS

- Saltwater fish cannot live in fresh water.
- Freshwater fish cannot live in salt water.
- A few fish can live in both fresh and salt water.
- Flatfish have flat bodies so they can rest on the seabed.

⬇ Piranhas swim in large shoals in South American rivers. They have very sharp teeth to eat other fish and occasionally large mammals.

Fish also live in tropical rivers, cool lakes, and icy mountain streams. They can live in almost any place where there is water.

↑ This peacock grouper lives mainly on coral reefs. It lies in wait for smaller fish, which it swallows whole.

← Angler fish live in deep parts of the oceans. They have a long, shiny nose-type feature that attracts smaller fish in the dark ocean depths.

Catching a Meal

The shape of a fish's mouth gives a clue to the type of food it eats. Predators, such as sharks and piranhas, have large mouths filled with pointed teeth.

← The great white shark has large pointed teeth, each tooth being 3 inches (7.5 cm) long. It eats the flesh of anything from fish to sea lions.

↓ This butterfly fish has a long, thin snout for catching food hiding in small cracks and between corals.

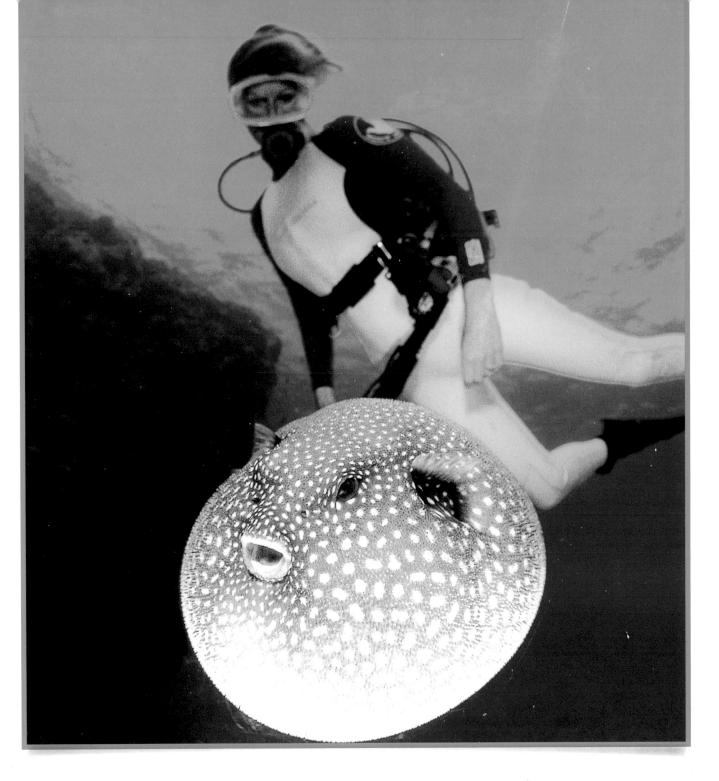

Fish that eat tiny sea creatures have a small mouth suitable for snapping up their food. Others, such as the queen trigger fish, have sharp chisel-like teeth to open the hard bodies of shellfish.

↑ The puffer fish inflates itself so that it appears too large for predators to eat.

← Catfish use their sensitive "whiskers" to find food. They eat mainly large fish.

Some fish feed by sucking up large mouthfuls of mud from the river bottom. They swallow the tiny creatures hiding in the mud and spit the rest out.

A few types of fish actually bury themselves in the sand on the seabed. They grab and eat any fish that gets too close.

FISH DEFENSES

- Most fish live in large shoals, or groups, which helps to protect them.
- Some fish have false eye spots to trick predators.
- Many fish are colored so that they blend into their surroundings.
- Some fish have poisonous spines.

↓ The lionfish is brightly colored, which warns other animals that it is poisonous.

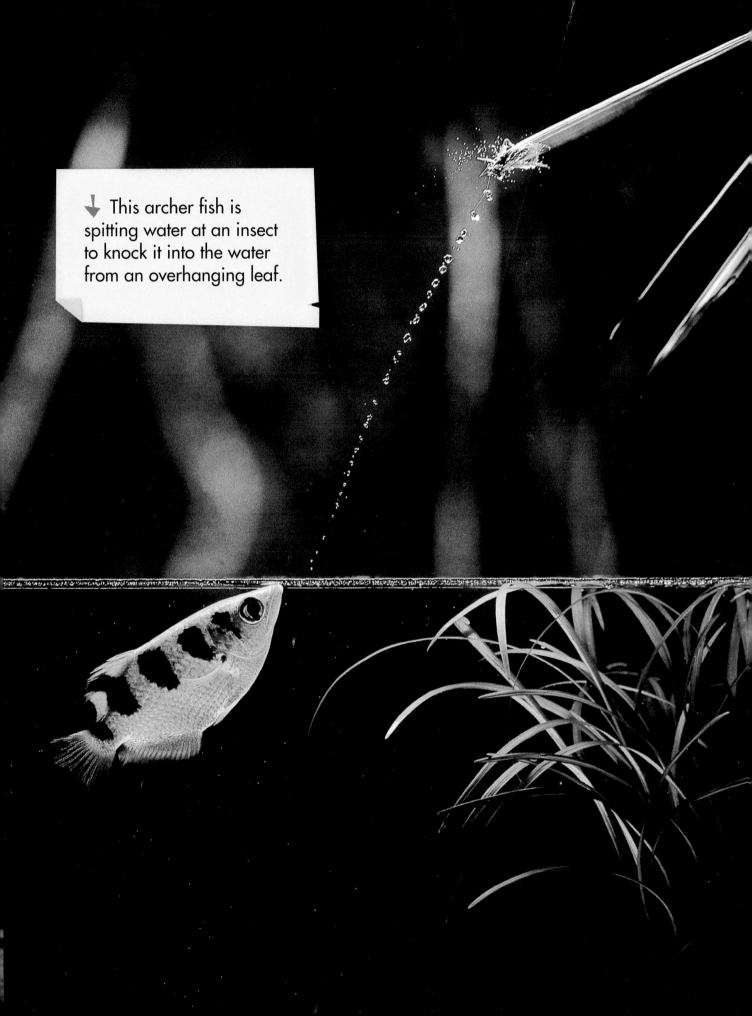

This archer fish is spitting water at an insect to knock it into the water from an overhanging leaf.

Hot and Cold

Fish live in oceans or rivers that are warm, cool, or cold. A fish that is used to living in a warm sea would die in a cold sea.

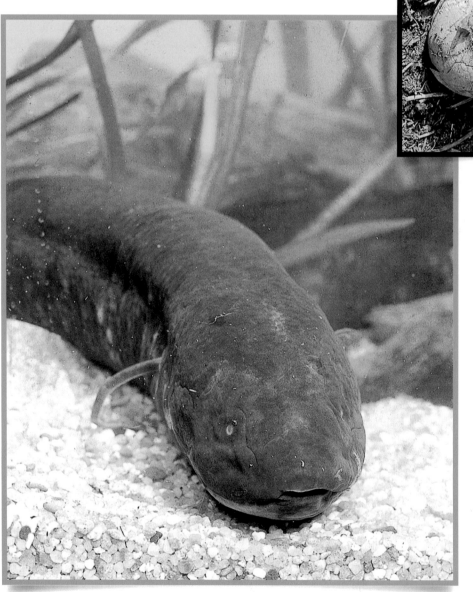

← This lungfish will survive even when there is no water in the river. (Above) When the river dries up, it will burrow into the mud, breathing with special lungs.

↑ A few types of fish live in pools that dry up in the dry season. This gardener's killifish may die, but its eggs will live and hatch when it rains again. (Inset) Killifish eggs hatching in a rain-filled pool.

A few types of fish live in some of the hottest and driest parts of the world. For some months of the year, there is no water at all.

The giant gorami lives in warm → water, which has less oxygen than cooler water. It survives by gulping air at the surface using a special lung.

In winter, when rivers and lakes become cold, fish rest near the bottom and hardly move until the water is warmer.

↓ In the winter, seashore fish like this common blenny may move to deeper water, which will be warmer.

HOW FISH COPE IN HOT AND COLD CONDITIONS

- Desert pupfish can live in water temperatures as hot as 122°F (50°C).

- Antarctic fish live in water temperatures as low as 28°F (-2°C).

- Some fish migrate to warmer climates.

↓ The icefish lives in the freezing waters of the Antarctic Ocean.

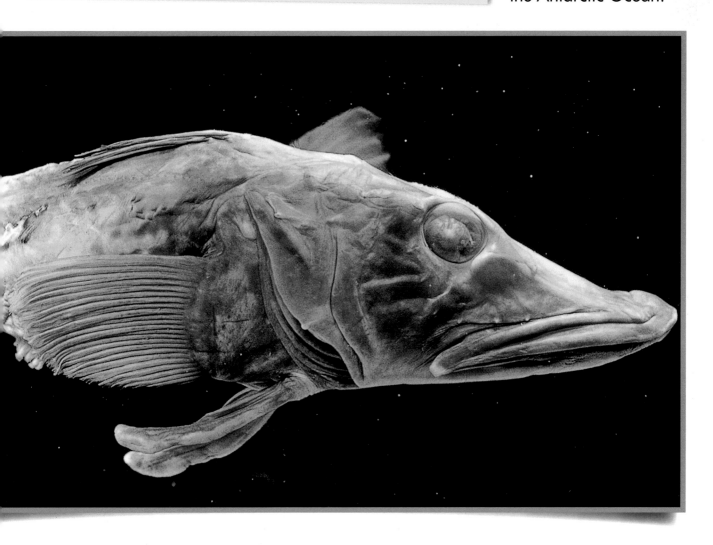

Fish living in Arctic and Antarctic waters can survive freezing temperatures. They produce a chemical that acts as an antifreeze to stop their blood freezing.

Getting Around

Most fish swim by moving their tails from side to side. The fins on the top and bottom of their bodies keep the fish upright.

⬆ Rays have large, winglike fins. These eagle rays swim using a graceful movement of their fins, or by gliding.

The sailfish is the fastest swimming fish. It can swim at a speed of 44 miles (70 km) per hour.

A fish uses the fins on the side of its body to steer itself. The faster a fish moves its tail from side to side, the faster it can swim.

The gurnard "walks" along the seabed on special feelers. It uses these feelers to find animals hiding under the sand.

Some fish hide in rocky holes during the day and come out at night to feed. Coral reefs and shipwrecks provide plenty of hiding places.

↓ The Moray eel lives in a deep rocky hole. It swims by rippling its long body.

MOVING AROUND

- Fish swim by moving their tails from side to side.
- Flying fish move their tails 50 beats a second to leap out of the water.
- Sharks have no swim bladder and will sink if they stop swimming.
- Seahorses can hover in the water.

← Mudskippers live in mangrove swamps. At low tide, they move around on the mud using leglike fins.

A few fish move differently from other fish. This includes gliding and even climbing out of the water in search of food.

↑ To escape predators, flying fish leap out of the sea and glide 33 feet (10 meters) or more. The flying fish's side fins are like wings.

Fish Young

Fish have developed different ways to make sure their young survive. Most fish lay eggs, but a few give birth to live young.

↓ Adult salmon live in the sea. To give birth, they return to the same river in which they hatched. There, the female lays thousands of tiny eggs.

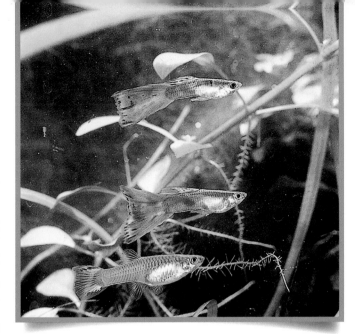

Most egg-laying fish lay thousands of eggs to make sure that some survive. Some sharks and rays lay fewer eggs, protected by a tough outer case. The young are larger than other newly hatched fish and less likely to be eaten.

↑ The female guppy (bottom, below two males) has eggs that hatch inside her body. The young swim away as soon as they are born.

↓ You can see the baby dogfish growing inside these egg cases. The yolks provide food while they grow.

Some fish stay with their eggs and protect them against predators. They attack other fish that come too close.

A few types of fish lay their eggs in a nest. Other fish protect their eggs and young in more unusual ways.

↑ Male parent seahorses have a special pouch in which they keep the eggs until they are ready to hatch.

← The male Siamese fighting fish makes a nest by blowing a lot of bubbles. He collects the eggs laid by the female and blows them into the nest.

FACTS ABOUT EGGS AND YOUNG FISH

- A female sunfish lays 300 million eggs at one time—more than any other fish.
- Some fish perform a courtship dance.
- Male fish are often more colorful than females.
- Some female wrasse can become males.

↓ Mouthbrooder cichlids carry their eggs in their mouth. The young fish return to the parent in times of danger.

Fish Pets

People often keep fish as pets because of their fascinating shapes, colors, and movement. Sometimes they are kept in garden ponds.

← A goldfish has all the features of a typical fish, including a line of tiny holes along the side of its body that allow it to pick up vibrations.

Sticklebacks live → in ponds and streams. They are sometimes caught and kept for a short time in a fish tank.

Fish can also be kept indoors in a fish tank. The tank should provide the same conditions for the fish as it would have in the wild.

↑ Some fish swim near the surface of ponds, while others live and feed near the bottom.

HOW TO TAKE CARE OF YOUR PET FISH

- Fish should be kept in a special fish tank. Some tanks have lids to protect the fish from harm.
- Grow water plants in the tank and place rocks and sand in the bottom.
- Feed your fish with the correct food.
- Make sure the water is kept clean.

Unusual Fish

⬆ The lamprey has no jaws. It attaches itself to a large bony fish with a sucker and feeds on its blood.

Most fish have a hard skeleton and bones. They are called "bony fish." Some fish, such as sharks and rays, have softer skeletons.

STRANGE FACTS

- Although flatfish, such as sole and plaice, can lie flat on the seabed, they are born upright like other fish.

- Cave fish live in dark caves and have no eyes.

- The four-eyed fish can see predators above the water and food beneath the water at the same time.

Bony fish may have very unusual features, including a sucker for sticking to rocks, or a body that looks like a rock. Some fish, such as the cleaner wrasse, live with other fish in a way that helps both fish.

↑ Can you see the tiny fish in this larger fish's mouth? The tiny fish is called a cleaner wrasse. It lives with the larger fish, eating parasites that live on its body and cleaning it at the same time.

← The colorful box fish has tiny little fins on either side of its cube-shaped body.

Scale of Fish

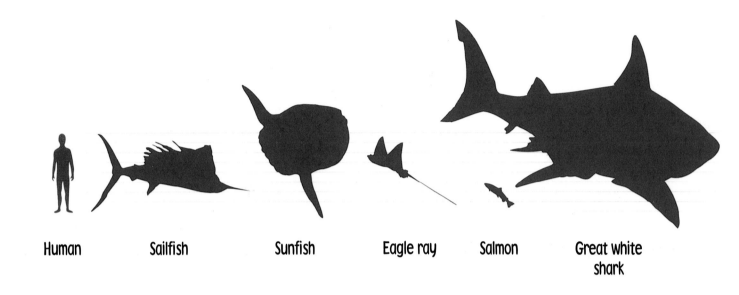

Human   Sailfish   Sunfish   Eagle ray   Salmon   Great white shark

Human hand   Lionfish   Mudskipper   Mouthbrooder cichlid   Piranha   Catfish

Human hand   Archer fish   Butterfly fish   Common blenny   Boxfish   Flying fish

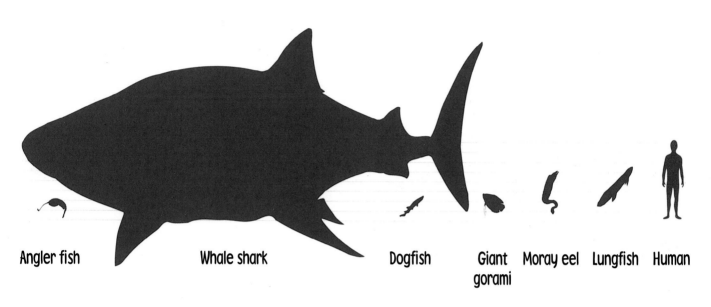

Angler fish   Whale shark   Dogfish   Giant   Moray eel   Lungfish   Human
                                                            gorami

Peacock   Puffer fish   Siamese   Seahorse   Three-   Cleaner   Human
grouper   fighting   spined   wrasse   hand
                                      fish   stickleback

Goldfish   Flying   Icefish   Killifish   Lamprey   Leafy sea   Human
                  gurnard   dragon   hand

Topic Web

SCIENCE
Classification.
Growth and reproduction.
How fish adapt to their environment.
Food chain.
Predators and prey.

GEOGRAPHY
Fish habitats—tropical, temperate, and polar seas; lakes, rivers, and streams.
Where do the fish we eat come from?

MATH
Measure and compare fish sizes with each other

ARTS & CRAFTS
Make a collage or paint a mural, showing fish in their habitats.

DRAMA/DANCE
Mime fish swimming around a coral reef. Show a predator hunting smaller fish.

ENGLISH
Imagine you are in a submarine, diving to the depths of the ocean. Describe what you see on the way down.

Activities

Science Study fish in an aquarium, pond, or fish tank. How do they spend their day? What food do they prefer? How do they rest?

English Imagine that you are in a submarine on its way to the dark ocean depths. Describe how the light changes as the submarine dives. Write about the various creatures you encounter. Or imagine you are a fish, perhaps a ray or shark. Describe your life.

Geography Draw a simple map of the world. Mark on it the seas, oceans, and main lakes and rivers. Show which fish live in these habitats. Look at the fish at a supermarket fish counter.

Which fish are caught in your state's waters and which come from another area? Draw a chart to show how fish are caught and how they get to the store.

Arts & Crafts Make a collage of a fish. Cut out the scales from colored paper and glue them on so that they overlap. Use tracing or tissue paper to make the transparent fish fins. Paint a scene of fish in their habitat.

Drama/Dance Create a mime or improvise a dance to show how different fish move, and how they rest and feed. You could show a shark circling and then attacking its prey.

Math Use the scale on pages 28–29 to compare the sizes of different fish with each other and with you, or with your hand.

Glossary

Antarctic The region at or around the South Pole.

Arctic The region at or around the North Pole.

Camouflage Protection from attack by appearing to be part of the surroundings.

Coral reef A ridge near the surface of the sea, formed in masses by the skeletons of tiny sea animals.

Courtship dance A dance performed to attract a mate.

Habitats The natural homes of plants and animals.

Hatch To produce young from eggs.

Hover To stay suspended, without moving forward.

Mangrove swamp An area covered with the roots of mangrove trees.

Migrate To move from one area to another to escape the cold.

Parasites Animals that live and feed on others.

Plankton Tiny creatures in water that are eaten by larger creatures.

Predators Animals that hunt others for food.

Shoals Groups of fish.

Skeleton The bony framework of the body of a fish or other animal.

Sucker An organ allowing an animal to cling to something by suction.

Swim bladder An air-filled sac that keeps fish afloat when they are not swimming.

Tropical To do with the tropics, the areas north and south of the equator.

Vibrations Tiny movements.

Finding Out More

Books to Read

The Best Book of Sharks by Clare Llewellyn (Kingfisher, 2005)

Simon & Schuster Children's Guide to Sea Creatures by Jinny Johnson (Simon & Schuster Children's Publishing, 1998)

About Fish (A Guide for Children) by Cathryn P. Sill and Jonathan Sill (Peachtree Publishers, 2005)

Websites

National Geographic Kids
http://kids.nationalgeographic.com/kids/animals/creaturefeature/
Click on Fish to learn all about these fascinating creatures and their habitats.

National Wildlife Federation
www.nwf.org/Wildlife/Wildlife-Library.aspx
Find out how your favorite fish live!

Index

Page numbers in **bold** refer to photographs.

Picture Acknowledgements:
Bruce Coleman 8(l), 9, 16, /Franco Banfi Title page, 4, 7(t), /Luiz Claudio Marigo 6, /Hans Reinhard 10(t), 12(b), /Andrew Purcell 17(b), /C. Lockwood 18, /Jane Burton 19(t), 21/ Jeff Foot Prod. 22 and title page (inset), 24(b), 25(t), /Hans Reinhard 26, /Bill Wood 27(b); FLPA /K. Aitken/Panda 5, /Frank Lane 13(b) and contents page, /D.P. Wilson 21(t), /Jeremy McCabe 23(t); NHPA /Norbert Wu 7(b), 8(r), /Trevor McDonald 10(b), /Stephen Dalton 11, /Daniel Heuclin 12(t), /Gerard Lacz 13(t), /14, /Laurie Campbell 15, Norbert Wu 17(t), 19(b), /B. & C. Alexander 20, /Anthony Bannister 23(b), /B. Jonks & M. Shimlock 27(t); Oxford Scientific Films /Max Gibbs Cover (inset), /E.R. Degginger 13t (inset); Shutterstock, cover picture; Wayland Picture Library 24(t), 25(b).
Artwork on pages 28–9 by Mark Whitchurch.